RESEARCH REPORT JANUARY 2016

Teacher Evaluation in Chicago

Differences in Observation and Value-Added Scores by Teacher, Student, and School Characteristics

Jennie Y. Jiang and Susan E. Sporte

TABLE OF CONTENTS

ACKNOWLEDGEMENTS

The authors gratefully acknowledge the Joyce Foundation for its ongoing support of this body of work surrounding the implementation and implications of the reform of Chicago Public Schools' (CPS) teacher evaluation system. Such long-term commitment has been vital as we have sought to understand and share the challenges, opportunities, and nuances of REACH Students.

We would also like to acknowledge the support of CPS and the Chicago Teachers Union (CTU). Our conversations and meetings with former and current directors of educator effectiveness at CPS, Paulette Poncelet and Michael Herring, and with manager Amanda Smith and with Carol Caref and Jennifer Johnson of the CTU have informed the content of this report, as have our interactions with other members of the CPS-CTU Joint Teacher Evaluation Committee. We also thank Christina Pagan, formerly with the Department of Performance Data and Policy, for providing insights into the intricacies of the data, and Stephen Ponisciak of the Wisconsin Center for Educational Research and Accountability for explanations about value added.

Many other members of the Chicago education community, representing a wide variety of viewpoints, have also helped to inform our understanding of the issues raised by this report as we have presented findings on a number of occasions, and we have appreciated their insights and commitment to the larger goal of improving education for all of Chicago's students. We thank our Steering Committee members for thoughtful comments, especially Veronica Anderson, Carol Caref, Lynn Cherkasky-Davis, Raquel Farmer-Hinton, and Luis Soria. Stuart Luppescu provided extremely helpful suggestions and technical advice throughout the entire analytic process. As always, colleagues from the University of Chicago Consortium on School Research (UChicago Consortium) have served as readers and thought partners as we conceptualized, analyzed, and wrote multiple drafts. We especially thank Elaine Allensworth, Joshua Klugman, Jenny Nagaoka, Marisa de la Torre, Kaleen Healey, Lauren Sartain, and Jen Cowhy for methodological, conceptual, and editorial suggestions. We thank former communications colleagues Cornelia Grumman and Emily Krone, as well as current staff members Bronwyn McDaniel and Jessica Puller from the Consortium and Lucinda Fickel from UChicago Urban Education Institute for their insightful feedback, support, and countless careful readings. Special thanks to Joshua Klugman, Paul Moore and Valerie Michelman for their expertise as technical readers and to research assistants Philip Carlitz and Julianna St. Onge for their invaluable support.

We also gratefully acknowledge the Spencer Foundation and the Lewis-Sebring Family Foundation, whose operating grants support the work of the Consortium.

This report was produced by UChicago Consortium's publications and communications staff: Bronwyn McDaniel, Director for Outreach and Communication; and Jessica Puller, Communications Specialist.

Graphic Design: Jeff Hall Design
Photography: Cynthia Howe
Editing: Ann Lindner

01.2016/pdf/jh.design@rcn.com

Executive Summary

This report is part of a series of studies on teacher evaluation in Chicago. Previous reports focused on implementation and on teacher and administrator perceptions of Chicago's new evaluation system. This report addresses differences in teacher observation and value-added scores across schools and how those scores are related to school and teacher characteristics.

In the fall of 2012, Chicago Public Schools (CPS) instituted a sweeping reform of its teacher evaluation system with the introduction of Recognizing Educators Advancing Chicago's Students (REACH). REACH replaces CPS's former 1970s-era evaluation system. This previous checklist system fell short in providing teachers meaningful feedback for improving their instructional practice as well as identifying which teachers excelled or which needed improvement. Over the course of only a few years, most districts across the nation have moved from similar checklist evaluation systems to new evaluation systems utilizing an evidenced-based observation rubric, a formal feedback process and measures of student growth in teachers' observations. These data provide additional information on individual teacher's practice as well as better information about the quality of a district's overall teaching workforce.

This report is part of a series of Consortium studies on teacher evaluation in Chicago. Previous reports focused on implementation and on teacher and administrator perceptions of REACH.[1] These reports found REACH has provided more differentiation among teachers and that most teachers and administrators had positive opinions about the new system, especially the observation process. Overwhelming majorities of teach-

ers and administrations believe the observation process supports teacher growth, identifies areas of strength and weaknesses, and provides opportunities for reflection. Teachers remain apprehensive, however, on the inclusion of student growth metrics in their evaluations.

REACH and other new evaluation systems have provided new data and information about the quality and distribution of the overall teaching workforce. With this new information it is now possible to gauge the degree to which different groups of students have equitable access to teachers with high scores using actual metrics of teaching practice rather than proxies for teaching quality such as scores on certification tests, experience, or degrees earned.

This report addresses differences in teacher observation and value-added scores across schools and how those scores are related to school and teacher characteristics. It provides a descriptive analysis of the relationship between teachers' evaluation scores and both school and individual teacher characteristics. It examines multiple sources of data from 2013-14, REACH's second year of implementation, including teacher observation scores and value-added scores, student demographic and test score data, survey responses, and teacher personnel data. These data represent the

---

1   Sporte, Stevens, Healey, Jiang, & Hart (2013); Jiang, Sporte, & Luppescu (2013); Jiang & Sporte (2014); Jiang, Sporte, & Luppescu (2015).

first fully comprehensive snapshot of evaluation scores for teachers in Chicago. For the first time, we have measures from observations for most of CPS's 19,000 teachers and individual value-added measures for those teachers teaching tested subjects and grades. By comparing the patterns of school and teacher characteristics on both observation and value-added scores this report begins to surface questions about the instruction experienced by Chicago's students, and about the degree to which individual measures of teacher effectiveness may be sensitive to school context or other external factors.

Key Findings

- **Schools serving the most disadvantaged students have an overrepresentation of teachers with the lowest value added and observation scores.** On both value-added and observation scores, teachers with the lowest scores are overrepresented in schools with the highest concentration of low-income students. This overrepresentation persists even after controlling for differences in teacher characteristics in high- and low-poverty schools such as experience levels.

- **Observation scores have a stronger relationship with school characteristics, such as the percentage of economically disadvantaged students, than value-added scores.** On observation scores, teachers in lower poverty schools have substantially higher scores on average than teachers in higher poverty schools. Differences on value added are much smaller as value-added measures explicitly control for student characteristics such as poverty and previous achievement. It is not clear whether this relationship exists because observations are reflecting differences in instruction in low and high poverty schools, or if it is harder to be effective or receive high observation ratings in a high-poverty school.

- **Teachers in schools with stronger organizational climates have higher evaluation scores.[2]** Teachers in schools with better organizational and learning climates tend to have higher value-added and observa-

tion scores. These differences remain significant when comparing schools with similar student populations.

- **There are some differences in teachers' evaluation scores, depending on experience and credentials.** Teachers with more experience have higher scores on value added and observations than new teachers. Differences between teachers with National Board Certification or advanced degrees, compared to those without those credentials, were found only on observation scores, not value added.

- **Minority teachers have lower observation scores than white teachers, but no significant differences on value added.** On average, minority teachers' observation scores were lower than white teachers' observation scores. However, a large proportion of this difference is due to the substantial relationship between observation scores and school characteristics, such as school-level poverty, as minority teachers are overrepresented in the highest-poverty schools and underrepresented in the lowest-poverty schools. There were no significant differences by teacher race/ethnicity on either reading or math value-added scores.

- **Male teachers have lower observation and value-added scores than female teachers.** On average, male teachers scored lower than female teachers on observations and slightly lower on value added than their female counterparts within the same schools.

While this report describes the relationships between teacher evaluation scores, their characteristics, and the context in which they teach, it does not explain why these relationships exist. Districts and states across the nation have found similar patterns in the relationship of teacher evaluation ratings with school poverty. There are many potential explanations for these patterns, and it is too soon to come to any conclusions about their source. Further research is needed to understand the degree to which observation scores, in particular, may be reflecting true differences in instructional practice or reflecting contextual factors, such as classroom or school composition.

---

2 As measured by the 5Essentials and Supplemental Survey Measures from the CPS 2014 *My Voice, My School* surveys.

Introduction

In the fall of 2012, Chicago Public Schools (CPS) instituted a reform of its teacher evaluation system with the introduction of REACH Students. This reform was part of an overall movement nationwide to improve how educators are assessed. These new systems have generated a wealth of data. This report uses CPS teacher evaluation data and begins to explore questions about students' access to effective teaching and the degree to which evaluation scores may be sensitive to student and school characteristics.

Decades of research evidence have consistently found that teachers are the most important in-school factor related to student learning and achievement. Students taught by an effective teacher have better academic outcomes, greater chances of post-secondary success, and higher lifetime earnings.[3] At the same time, there are many unresolved questions about how to measure effective teaching, how to develop effective teachers, and how to ensure that all students have access to highly effective teaching. These issues continue to be among the most persistent challenges facing local, state, and federal education policymakers.

Policymakers at the federal level have attempted to both improve teacher quality and address inequities in students' access to effective teachers. In 2001, the federal government attempted to address inequities in students' access to effective teachers by monitoring their qualifications. The No Child Left Behind (NCLB) act of 2001 required states to ensure all teachers met minimum certification standards.[4] Beginning in 2009, the federal Race to the Top funding incentivized states to overhaul their teacher evaluation systems, with the premise that better evaluation policies and systems could be a primary vehicle for improving teaching and learning across schools.[5] That federal focus continues as states have been given opportunities to pursue waivers, exempting them from some components of NCLB. In exchange for flexibility in other areas, they are required to describe their evaluation systems and commit to timelines for evaluation system design and implementation.

Within the Last Decade, Teacher Evaluation Has Taken Center Stage in Policy Reform Efforts

In response to federal policies and incentives, the landscape for teacher evaluation policies and practices has undergone rapid and dramatic change. As of 2013, thirty-five states now require the inclusion of student achievement measures in their teacher evaluations and more than half of states require annual evaluations of all teachers.[6] Although states and districts vary considerably in the measures they use and the weights those measures are given, most now include observations of teacher practice and measures of student growth as part of a combined final evaluation score. And, although states and districts are taking different approaches to implementing these teacher evaluation systems, they commonly aim to improve teacher effectiveness

---

3   Aaronson, Barrow, & Sander (2007); Chetty, Friedman, & Rockoff (2013); Goldhaber (2002); Rockoff (2004); Rivkin, Hanushek, & Kain (2005).
4   U.S. Department of Education (2001).
5   U.S. Department of Education (2009).
6   Steinberg & Donaldson (2014); National Council on Teacher Quality (2013).

through two key levers: 1) developing teachers' instructional skills through focused feedback, professional development, and incentives for improvement and 2) holding teachers accountable by incorporating evaluation measures into personnel decisions such as tenure and dismissal.

These new evaluation systems have brought both opportunities and challenges. For example, teachers and principals believe the new evaluation process is leading to changes in teacher practice and improved communication and collaboration.[7] In Chicago, overwhelming majorities of administrators and two-thirds of teachers agree that the observation process will lead to better instruction.[8] There is also limited, but promising, evidence that the use of evidence-based observations improves instructional practice, as well as student learning.[9] At the same time, districts and states have described challenges related to developing and using evaluation measures and building capacity and sustainability.[10] Teachers remain apprehensive about the inclusion of student growth metrics in their evaluations, and both teachers and administrators report increased levels of stress related to evaluation.[11] Despite these tensions, many districts and states have embraced teacher evaluation as a component of their improvement strategy.

Data From New Evaluation Systems Allows Us to Explore Questions About Equity for Teachers and Students

Over the course of only a few years, most districts have moved from an annual checklist conveying little information on teacher performance to detailed reports including evaluation data from multiple classroom observations and measures of student growth.[12] These data not only provide additional information on individual teachers' practice, but also provide better information about the quality of the district's overall

teaching workforce. Examining the distribution of teachers' scores and ratings may give insight into how teachers are deployed across a district and the nature of instruction received by students.

Past research has repeatedly shown that economically disadvantaged and minority students are more likely to be taught by inexperienced teachers with lower qualifications, as well as those who have lower value-added scores.[13] New evaluation systems provide the opportunity to assess teaching, using a broader range of information on instructional quality across the district. It is now possible to gauge the degree to which different groups of students have equitable access to high-scoring teachers, using actual metrics of teaching

---

7   Jiang & Sporte (2014); Murphy, Cole, Pike, Ansaldo, & Robinson (2014); Sporte et al. (2013).
8   Jiang & Sporte (2014).
9   Steinberg & Sartain (2015); Taylor & Tyler (2013); Grissom, Loeb, & Master (2013).
10 Government Accountability Office (2013).
11 Jiang et al. (2014); Sporte et al. (2013).

12 Many also use student perception measures, such as student surveys, and other measures of teacher practice, such as student learning objectives.
13 Lankford, Loeb, & Wyckoff (2002); Clotfelter, Ladd, & Vigdor (2006); Goldhaber, Lavery, & Theobald (2015); DeAngelis, Presley, & White (2005).

practice, including observations of classroom teaching rather than proxies for teaching quality derived from teacher qualifications or certification test scores. It is also now possible to compare and contrast patterns from multiple measures of teacher performance such as observations and value-added scores.

These data also allow us to investigate the relationship between teacher characteristics and their evaluation scores. In Chicago and elsewhere, the overall teaching workforce has become whiter and less experienced.[14] This is of concern, as research has found that minority teachers tend to have higher expectations for minority students and have positive effects on their academic achievement.[15] If groups of teachers—novice teachers, teachers with advanced certification, or teachers of one race or gender—have systematically higher or lower evaluation scores than their peers, then school and district administrators may need to pay special attention to how these groups of teachers are supported. We can also determine whether markers of teacher quality that are used in the hiring process, including experience and National Board Certification, are related to teachers' effectiveness ratings. This information could be useful to administrators deciding how strongly to consider these types of qualifications during the hiring process.

While the new measures are likely to improve the identification of schools with more effective teaching practices, there are still questions about whether they can fairly assess individual teacher quality. That is, it is not clear whether all teachers have an equal opportunity to receive strong ratings. There is emerging research on teacher evaluation systems that finds teachers of students with higher prior achievement systematically receive higher observation scores, thus creating an uneven playing field for educators teaching students with lower achievement.[16] A system that makes it more difficult for teachers working in challenging contexts to achieve high ratings could have adverse consequences for equity

for both students and teachers. It may lead to effective teachers avoiding teaching in schools where strong teaching practices are most needed, and it may penalize those teachers who do decide to work in those contexts.

By using multiple metrics of teaching effectiveness, we can compare teachers' ratings on value added scores—which compare gains for students with similar backgrounds and prior achievement—to their ratings on observation metrics—which do not have adjustments for the types of students in a teacher's classroom. This could particularly be an issue if certain kinds of teachers are more likely to teach in contexts where it is difficult to get a strong rating. This is particularly a concern for groups that are underrepresented in the teacher workforce, including minority teachers and male teachers.

This report presents a descriptive analysis of the relationships of teacher ratings with the context in which they teach, but it does not discern the reasons why the relationships exist. Understanding the extent to which there are systematic differences in teacher ratings across different types of schools is only the first step for addressing possible inequities for students and teachers. Once we understand the extent of systematic differences, then we can examine the reasons they exist and potential ways to address them in future studies.

This report shows the distribution of the observation and value-added scores across schools, and how they are related to school and teacher characteristics. It addresses the following questions:

1. To what extent are measures of teacher effectiveness (value-added and observation scores) related to the characteristics of students in schools?

- Are measures of effectiveness related to the level of student poverty in schools?

- Are these relationships different for value-added and observation scores?

5

---

14 Moore (2015, July 14); Albert Shanker Institute (2015).

15 Dee (2005); Ferguson (2003); Egalite, Kisida, & Winters (2015).

16 Whitehurst, Chingos, & Lindquist (2014); Steinberg & Garrett (forthcoming).

- Do teachers with more years of experience have higher value-added and/or observation scores? What about teachers with advanced degrees or National Board Certification?

- Are there differences in REACH scores by teachers' race or gender?

- To what extent are any differences explained by differences in school characteristics?

This Study Extends Prior Research on Effective Teaching

The data set examined in this study represents the first fully comprehensive snapshot of observation scores for teachers in Chicago. For the first time, we have measures from observations for most of CPS's 19,000 teachers and individual value-added measures for those teachers teaching tested subjects in grades 3-8. Thus we can begin to examine to what extent Chicago's patterns of teacher quality align with or differ from what research has found elsewhere.

This study builds the knowledge base of what is known about measures of teaching effectiveness in a number of ways. Most of the prior research has only examined relationships between school characteristics and teacher effectiveness, as measured by teacher qualifications (e.g., education level or experience) or value-added scores; this study explores patterns in observation scores, as well as value-added scores and teacher qualification metrics. Observation scores are available for a much broader range of teachers than value-added scores, which are only calculated for teachers of particular subjects in particular grades. They also directly capture differences in students' experiences in the classroom, rather than indirectly capturing the effects of the classroom on students' test scores. Yet, because observation scores are not adjusted for differences in students' characteristics, they may also be influenced by the characteristics of schools and classrooms more so than the value-added metrics. Comparing the patterns of school and teacher characteristics on two measures, observation and value-added scores, allows us to capture different dimensions of these patterns and may also begin to surface questions about whether either measure may be sensitive to school context or other external factors.

Data Used for This Study

REACH evaluation scores are a combination of professional practice—measured by observation ratings—and student growth. Ratings from four observations, conducted by principals or assistant principals who have been trained and certified on the rubric, make up the professional practice score. Observation ratings are based on the CPS Framework for Teaching, a modified version of the Danielson Framework for Teaching. Ratings include 19 components, based on four domains of practice; *Planning and Preparation, Classroom Environment, Instruction,* and *Professional Responsibilities.*[17]

Student growth includes two different metrics, value-added scores and performance tasks.[18] Student growth totals are combined in different ways, based on a teacher's grade and subject. Most teachers get a value-added score—either an individual score if they teach in tested subjects and grades, or a school-wide literacy score if they teach in non-tested subjects or grades. Teachers also receive a score based on student growth on performance tasks, assessments created by teams of teachers, and district-level content specialists. There are grade- and subject-specific performance tasks covering virtually all grades and subjects.

Evaluation scores carry consequences for both tenured and non-tenured teachers. A teacher's summative REACH rating is tied directly to the district's dismissal, remediation, and tenure attainment policies.[19]

In this report, we use 2013-14 data from a number of sources, including CPS administrative data, CPS REACH teacher evaluation data, and responses of students and teachers to the *My Voice, My School* Survey.

CPS Schools 2013-14	
Elementary Schools	425
High Schools	101
Total Number of Schools	526

Note: Only schools with REACH data in 2013-14 were included in our analyses and reflected in the numbers above. Charter schools do not utilize REACH and are not included in analyses.

2013-14 REACH Evaluation Data

REACH teacher evaluation data utilized in this report are from 2013-14 evaluation ratings of teachers.[20] Analyses of observation scores include non-tenured teachers and tenured teachers with observation ratings from at least two observations during the 2013-14 school year. The analyses only include teachers who were rated using the CPS Framework for Teaching. Librarians, counselors, clinicians, and other education support specialists rated on a different framework were not included in the analyses. Charter schools do not utilize REACH and are not included in our analyses.

Number of Teachers with REACH Evaluation Scores 2013-14		
Teacher School Level and Tenure Status	Number of Teachers with at Least Two Observations	Number of Teachers with Individual Value-Added Scores
Elementary Non-Tenured Teachers	3,706	1,173
Elementary Tenured Teachers	9,328	3,763
High School Non-Tenured Teachers	1,284	
High School Tenured Teachers	3,648	

Note: Only teachers with ratings from at least two observations were included in our analyses of observations. In 2013-14, about 94 percent of teachers (out of 19,098 total teachers in our dataset) had ratings from at least two observations.

---

17 See Appendix B for the CPS Framework for Teaching.
18 See Appendix A and Appendix B for more details on REACH.
19 Chicago Public Schools (2014).

20 For more details about REACH measures and their correlations, see Jiang et al. (2014).

CPS utilizes a variety of scales to report observation and value-added measures. In this report, for both value-added and observation scores, we utilize the 100 to 400 point scale used by CPS for overall professional practice and student growth scores for ease of comparison.

Throughout this report, *observation scores* refer to the overall professional practice scores for teachers, calculated using a weighted average of component ratings. *Observation ratings* refer to the four-level rating scale of the CPS Framework for Teaching (*Unsatisfactory, Developing, Proficient, Distinguished*).[21] In 2013-14, observations comprised 75 percent of a teacher's overall REACH score.[22]

Value-Added Scores refer to the individual value-added scores received by teachers in grades 3-8, teaching reading or math. In this report, we utilize multi-year averages (from 2012-13 and 2013-14) if teachers had value-added scores from both years available. Value-added scores are based on student results from the NWEA-MAP test, an adaptive, computer-based test.

Analyses of value-added scores in this report include only elementary teachers who received individual value-added scores. In 2013-14, high school teachers teaching ninth- through eleventh-grade tested subjects received an individual value-added score. However this value-added score only counted for 5 percent of their overall REACH score and, in 2014-15, no value-added scores were included in high school teachers' REACH ratings.

Student growth also includes a score based on performance tasks. These are written or hands-on assessments developed by teams of CPS teachers and central office staff and are designed to measure the mastery or progress toward mastery of a particular skill or standard. In both 2012-13 and 2013-14, we found little variation on teachers' performance task scores[23] and thus did not include analyses on performance tasks in this report.

2013-14 CPS Administrative Data

To examine equity of ratings across different types of schools, we aggregated CPS administrative student data to the school level, including students' race, previous achievement and their free/reduced-price lunch status. Measures of the economic status of students in schools were also derived from census data on students' residential neighborhoods, measured at the census block group level. A measure of poverty captured the percent of adult males unemployed and the percent of families with incomes below the poverty line.

2014 *My Voice, My School* Survey

Chicago students in grades 6-12 and all teachers and principals have been responding to surveys developed by UChicago Consortium since 1991. Most of the survey content is organized around the Five Essentials for School Improvement.[24] This report uses teachers' perceptions of their school's leadership, professional capacity, and parent support and students' perceptions of instruction and learning climate from the 2014 *My Voice, My School* survey as indicators of their school's organizational strength. For teachers, the response rate was 81 percent; for students, the overall response rate was 79 percent.

Observation and Value-Added Scores 2013-14					
	Average Score	Standard Deviation	Minimum	Maximum	Number of Teachers
Observations	309.44	48.28	100	400	17,966
Reading Value Added	249.66	40.78	100	400	4,106
Math Value Added	250.88	44.49	100	400	3,399

Note: For both value-added and observation scores, we utilize the 100 to 400 point scale used by CPS for overall professional practice and student growth scores for ease of comparison. In this report, we utilized multi-year averages (from 2012-13 and 2013-14) if teachers had value-added scores from both years.

---

21 See Appendix B for the CPS Framework for Teaching.
22 See Appendix A for details on percentages of each measure.

23 Jiang et al. (2014).
24 Bryk, Sebring, Allensworth, Luppescu, & Easton (2010).

CHAPTER 1

The Relationship between School Characteristics and REACH Scores

In this chapter, we explore how teachers' observation and value-added scores are distributed across schools. Prior research in Chicago and elsewhere has consistently shown that high-poverty schools tend to have more novice teachers and fewer teachers with stronger qualifications in terms of teacher test scores and certification.[25] Here, we investigate the relationship between school characteristics and teacher value-added and observation scores. In addition, we describe how teachers' evaluation scores differ by their school's organizational strength.

We present results for elementary schools, as we can present both observations and value-added scores. Findings on high school observations were similar to those for elementary schools and can be found in **Figure D.3**.

Teachers with the lowest value-added and observation scores are overrepresented in schools that serve the most disadvantaged students. On both value-added and observation scores, teachers with the lowest scores are overrepresented in schools serving the highest concentration of students in poverty. **Figures 1.A and 1.B** show how teachers with the highest and lowest scores on value added and observations are distributed among schools of varying poverty levels. If teacher ratings were evenly distributed across schools at all levels of student poverty, we would expect 20 percent of teachers with the lowest ratings to be at each level of student poverty; we would also expect that 20 percent of teachers with the highest ratings would be in schools at each level of student poverty.

Teacher scores are not evenly distributed across schools. The lowest-scoring teachers on both observation and value-added measures are more likely to be in schools with the greatest concentration of poverty. For example, of the teachers with the lowest scores on value added, 26 percent are in schools with the highest levels of poverty while only 13 percent are in schools with lowest concentration of poverty **(see Figure 1.A)**.

The differences in observation scores by school poverty level are more pronounced. Of the teachers with the lowest scores on observation ratings, 30 percent are in schools with the highest poverty while only 9 percent are in schools with lowest poverty **(see Figure 1.B)**.[26]

Teachers with the highest scores on observations are vastly underrepresented in highest-poverty schools; teachers with highest scores on value added are more evenly distributed across schools. Next we turn our attention from the lowest-scoring teachers to the highest-scoring teachers—those with the top 20 percent

---

Why Might We See Differences between Observations and Value-Added Scores?

Observation ratings are meant to capture a teacher's level of instructional practice in a classroom. An evaluator observes a classroom and captures evidence of a teacher's practice. This evidence is then utilized to assign ratings. Observation ratings do not control for any student or school characteristics.

Value-added estimates are intended to capture students' growth on test scores. Value-added estimates are constructed so that they explicitly control for measurable student characteristics such as gender, race/ethnicity, economic disadvantage, English learner, disability, and mobility, as well as prior test scores. This is meant to compare a teacher's students to similar students districtwide.

---

25 Lankford et al. (2002); Clotfelter et al. (2005); Goldhaber (2015); DeAngelis et al. (2005).
26 All analyses on observation scores conducted in this report were also replicated using the subsample of teachers with individual value-added scores. Results were similar to the full sample of teachers.

9

FIGURE 1

Teachers with Lowest Value-Added and Observation Scores are Over Represented in Schools Serving the Most Disadvantaged Students

FIGURE 1.A

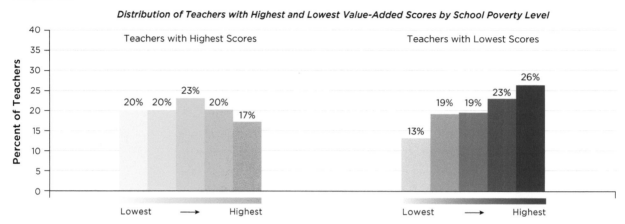

Distribution of Teachers with Highest and Lowest Value-Added Scores by School Poverty Level

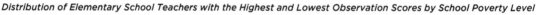

FIGURE 1.B

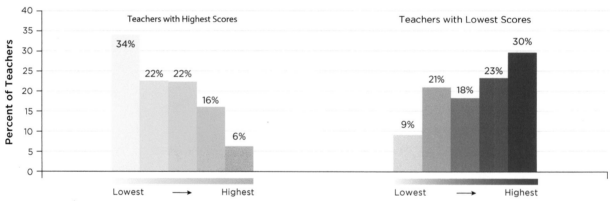

Distribution of Elementary School Teachers with the Highest and Lowest Observation Scores by School Poverty Level

Note: We ranked elementary and high schools by the percentage of students receiving free/reduced-price lunch. After ranking schools, we divided them into five equal-sized groups (quintiles), with the first quintile representing the lowest-poverty schools and the fifth quintile the highest-poverty schools. Both figures represent elementary school teachers only. Value-added scores include teachers in grades 3-8 reading and math only. There were 1,089 teachers with lowest value-added scores and 915 teachers with highest value-added scores. There were 2,609 teachers with lowest observation scores and 2,594 teachers with highest observation scores.

Measures of School Characteristics

School-level measures of student economic disadvantage, minority students, and prior achievement are highly related. In this report, we present relationships between REACH scores and school-level poverty because it is one of the biggest determinants of student outcomes and many policy interventions are motivated to reduce gaps in performance between low-income and other students.

Relationships between teacher evaluation scores and school-level percentages of minority students and achievement were similar to our findings with school-level poverty. Examples of these are provided in Appendix C.

Chicago is not the only district that has found relationships between teacher evaluation scores and school or student characteristics. Districts and states across the nation are finding similar trends. These include the following:

- **Washington, DC:** Teachers in low-poverty schools had higher IMPACT results than teachers in medium- and high-poverty schools.[A]

- **Minneapolis:** Schools with student populations of higher poverty had larger concentrations of teachers with scores below average.[B]

- **Washington State:** Measures of teacher quality, such as experience, licensure exam scores, and value-added estimates of effectiveness, are inequitably distributed across every indicator of student disadvantage—free/reduced-price lunch status, underrepresented minority, and low prior academic performance.[C]

- **Florida and North Carolina:** The average effectiveness of teachers as measured by value added in high-poverty schools is, in general, less than teachers at other schools, but only slightly. High-poverty schools also have much larger within-school variation.[D]

A   Education Consortium for Research and Evaluation (2013).
B   Matos (2015).
C   Goldhaber et al. (2015).
D   Sass, Hannaway, Xu, Figlio, & Feng (2010).

of observation scores. Only 6 percent of teachers with the highest observation scores teach in the highest-poverty schools, while 34 percent are in schools with lowest poverty. Thus, in the highest-poverty schools, not only are students more likely to be taught by teachers with the bottom scores on observations, they are also the least likely to be taught by teachers who have the top scores.

However, the prevalence of teachers with highest value-added scores is about even across schools with differing concentrations of economically disadvantaged students. As **Figure 1.A** shows, of teachers with top scores on value added, 20 percent teach in the lowest-poverty schools and 17 percent teach in highest-poverty schools.[27]

Differences in evaluation scores between high- and low-poverty schools persist even after controlling for differences in teacher experience and credentials. Differences in teacher credentials or experience levels between teachers in high- and low-poverty schools is one possible explanation for why teachers with lower evaluation scores tend to be in high-poverty schools. In CPS in 2013-14, higher-poverty schools had higher percentages of new teachers and lower percentages of

teachers with National Board Certification.[28] However, our findings in **Table 1** show that teacher experience and credentials do not explain the distribution of teacher observation and value-added scores among schools, as background characteristics account for only a small amount of the difference in both value-added or observation scores.

On value-added, top-scoring teachers in highest-poverty schools have higher scores than their counterparts in lower-poverty schools. On average, teacher value-added tends to be greater in low-poverty schools than in high-poverty schools. This average hides some surprising differences. Looking closer at the distribution of scores within higher- and lower-poverty schools, we find that the teachers with the highest value added in the high-poverty schools out score teachers with the highest value added in lower-poverty schools **(see Figure 2).**

There are distinct differences when comparing top, bottom, and middle scoring teachers in higher-poverty schools to their counterparts in lower-poverty schools. The teachers with the smallest value added among

27 Value-added scores displayed here depict individual value-added scores from 2012-13 and 2013-14 because multi-year averages were utilized where available. Individual value-added scores include combined scores for teachers teaching math and/or reading in grades 3-8. For distributions of teachers with highest and lowest scores, broken down by reading and math value added, see Appendix D.

28 See Appendix E for percentages of first-year teachers and NBCTs by school poverty level.

TABLE 1

Average Evaluation Scores by School Poverty Level

School Poverty Level	Observations		Value-Added Reading		Value-Added Math	
	Average Score (SD)	Controlling for Teacher Background	Average Score (SD)	Controlling for Teacher Background	Average Score (SD)	Controlling for Teacher Background
1-Lowest	332 (42)	331	256 (34)	256	251 (41)	251
2	312 (49)	308	254 (41)	252	251 (47)	252
3	312 (48)	305	256 (45)	258	255 (51)	256
4	304 (48)	298	247 (48)	250	248 (49)	251
5-Highest	289 (44)	288	246 (51)	247	248 (54)	249

Note: We ranked elementary and high schools by the percentage of students receiving free/reduced-price lunch. After ranking schools, we divided them into five equal-sized groups (quintiles), with the first quintile representing the lowest-poverty schools and the fifth quintile the highest-poverty schools.

The numbers in the "Controlling for teacher background" column represent average scores of teachers controlling for teacher characteristics including experience, advanced degrees, National Board Certification, and gender. This allows us to control for differences in teacher composition at schools. For example, some schools may have more first-year teachers than other schools.

FIGURE 2

Top-Scoring Teachers in Highest-Poverty Schools Have Higher Value-Added Scores than Their Counterparts in Lower-Poverty Schools

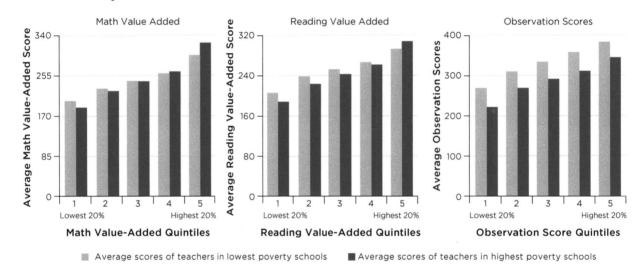

■ Average scores of teachers in lowest poverty schools　■ Average scores of teachers in highest poverty schools

How to Read Figure 2: In each graph, the purple bar on the right of each pair of bars represents the average scores of teachers in highest-poverty schools along each quintile of the distribution of teacher scores, while the orange bar on the left of each pair of bars represents the average scores of teachers in the lowest-poverty schools. For example, on each graph, the orange bar at the very left (quintile 1) is the average score of teachers in lowest-poverty schools with the bottom 20 percent of scores and the purple bar to the right is the average score of teachers in highest-poverty schools with the bottom 20 percent of scores. On each graph, the purple bar at the very right (quintile 5) represents the average score of teachers in the highest-poverty schools with the top scores among teachers in highest-poverty schools and the orange bar to the left of it represents the average scores of teachers in the lowest-poverty schools.

On observation scores, the difference between average scores of teachers is about 40 points along all quintiles. The gap between teachers' scores in the highest- and lowest-poverty schools is about the same for lowest-, highest-, and middle-scoring teachers. On value added reading and math, we see a gap in scores between teachers in higher- and lower-poverty scores only among the lower-scoring teachers. This gap is smaller than what we see on observations and not only does it narrow as one moves up the distribution of teacher scores, it disappears. In fact, on value added, the highest-scoring teachers in the highest-poverty schools have on average higher scores than their counterparts in lower-poverty schools.

Averages along the distribution were calculated separately for highest- and lowest-poverty schools.

teachers in lower-poverty schools (bottom 20 percent) score better than their counterparts in the higher-poverty schools. This narrows, closes, and reverses as one moves up the distribution of teacher value-added scores. On both reading and math value added, the top-scoring teachers in highest-poverty schools have higher scores than their counterparts in lower-poverty schools. Thus on value added reading and math, the average differences in scores between higher- and lower-poverty schools are driven by the lower scores of teachers at the lower end of the distribution.

On observation scores, the difference between average scores of teachers at low-poverty versus high-poverty schools is about 40 points (of the 100 to 400 point scale) along all quintiles of teachers. In other words, the teachers in the top 20 percent of observation scores in higher-poverty schools still score substantially less than teachers in the top 20 percent among teachers in low-poverty schools on the observation rubric.

In some schools, almost all observation ratings assigned are Proficient or Distinguished; in others, half are Basic or Unsatisfactory. There is a moderate negative correlation (-0.33) between observation scores and the concentration of economically disadvantaged students in schools.[29] On average, as the percentage of low-income students in a school increase, observation scores decrease. Observation scores are comprised of ratings of teaching practice assigned by evaluators and based on the standards described in the CPS Framework. There are four such rating categories: Distinguished, Proficient, Basic, and Unsatisfactory. **Figure 3** shows the percentage of each observation ratings in each school in 2013-14. In some schools, most ratings assigned were Distinguished (on the left end of the figure) and in some schools most ratings were Basic or lower (on the right end of the graph).

The schools with lower percentages of Proficient and Distinguished ratings on **Figure 3** tend to be higher-poverty schools. In fact, about 63 percent of schools with the lowest percentages of Proficient and

Should All Schools Have the Same Percentages of Ratings?

Teachers are not randomly assigned to schools. Therefore, we would not expect all schools to have the exact same percentages of assigned Distinguished or Unsatisfactory ratings, nor the exact same distribution on value added.

Some schools might have a high percentage of Distinguished teachers through recruitment or professional development efforts, or some schools might have a high percentage of teachers with Basic ratings because they have many teachers who are struggling or high rates of teacher attrition.

Distinguished ratings were higher-poverty schools (schools in the top two quintiles of school poverty).

The relationship between school poverty and observation ratings is similar when the ratings are broken down into each of the four domains of the CPS Framework for Teaching.[30] This moderate relationship of observation ratings with school poverty is not driven by one particular domain having a stronger relationship with school poverty.[31] In other words, teachers in low-poverty schools tend to have higher ratings on all aspects of teacher practice that are measured with the observation protocol—*Planning and Preparation, Classroom Environment, Instruction,* and *Professional Responsibilities*—compared to teachers in high-poverty schools. It is not just one domain of the rubric driving these relationships.

On both observations and value-added metrics, most of the variation in scores was among teachers within the same school, rather than across schools. The associations between observation and value-added scores and school-level poverty reflect overall averages of school-level scores. However, as shown in **Figure 3**, within most schools, there are some Distinguished ratings, some Proficient ratings, some Basic ratings, and some Unsatisfactory ratings.

13

---

29 See Table C.4 in Appendix C for correlations.
30 See Appendix B for details on these domains.

31 Domain averages are strongly correlated with each other. See Table C.4 in Appendix C for correlations for each domain.

FIGURE 3

Schools Varied in the Percentages of Unsatisfactory, Developing, Proficient, and Distinguished Ratings Assigned in 2013-14

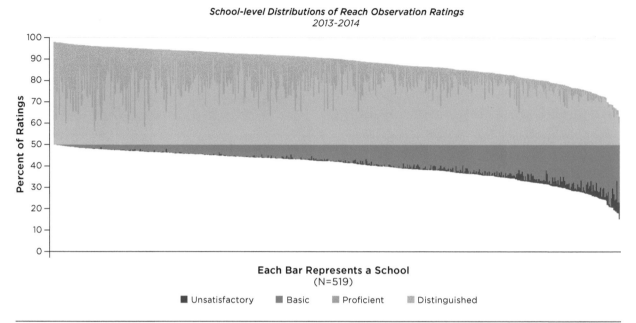

School-level Distributions of Reach Observation Ratings
2013-2014

Each Bar Represents a School
(N=519)

■ Unsatisfactory ■ Basic ■ Proficient ■ Distinguished

Note: Each bar represents a school and the percentage of Unsatisfactory, Basic, Proficient, and Distinguished ratings assigned to teachers in the school in the 2013-14 school year. Schools with fewer than 10 teachers were excluded. Includes only teachers rated on the teacher framework. Percentages are from 519 schools, 19,087 teachers and 6,069,069 observation ratings on 19 components.

In fact, as is the case in the observation ratings, there are greater differences in teachers' observation scores among teachers in the *same* school than there are among teachers in *different* schools. About two-thirds of the total difference across teachers' observation scores is due to differences among teachers in the same school; this is the case for almost three-quarters of the difference among teachers' value-added scores. In any given school—high- or low-poverty—there are teachers with very high, low, or average scores on observations and teachers with very high, low, or average scores on value added.

In schools with stronger culture and climate, teachers have higher scores on both value added and observations. Prior research has suggested that it might be easier to be an effective teacher in a school that has a strong climate and organization—where school leadership is strong and trusted, teachers feel committed to their

job, and students show strong academic behaviors.[32] We examined relationships between the climate and culture of schools and the observation and value-added scores of teachers in those schools utilizing student and teacher perceptions of climate and culture from the district-wide *My Voice, My School* surveys from the spring of 2014. In schools with stronger professional climate—as perceived by teachers—and stronger learning climate and instruction—as perceived by students— teachers tend to have higher scores on both value-added and observation scores.[33] **Figure 4** depicts the relationships between a few key measures of school climate and culture and teachers' observation, reading value-added and math value-added scores.[34] For example, the difference in teachers' observation scores between schools with average school commitment and schools with very strong school commitment is 8.1 points.[35] On math value added the difference is 3.1 points, and on reading

---

32 Sebastian & Allensworth (2012).

33 Controlling for school-level characteristics such as poverty and prior achievement. See Appendix F for complete regression tables and details on analysis.

34 See Appendix F for more information about our surveys and our measures of school climate and culture.

35 Coefficients represent a one standard deviation difference in a school's climate measure.

FIGURE 4

Relationship between Measures of School Climate and REACH Scores

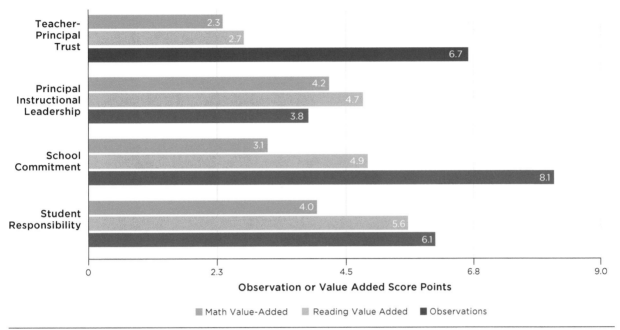

Observation or Value Added Score Points

■ Math Value-Added   ■ Reading Value Added   ■ Observations

Note: Results are coefficients from regressions run separately to avoid collinearity issues and depict a one standard deviation change on measures of school climate and culture. A one standard deviation difference on a measure is similar to comparing a "Below Average" to an "Average" school on that measure or comparing an "Average" school to an "Above Average" school on that measure. We analyzed many measures of school climate and present four here as examples. Results from all measures can be found in Table F.1 in Appendix F.

value added the difference is 4.9 points.[36]

While relationships between evaluation scores and measures of culture and climate are significant, what remains unknown is whether a strong school culture facilitates strong teaching, whether schools with strong culture are better at recruiting effective teachers, or whether high-scoring teachers themselves are creating an environment with strong culture and climate.

---

36 For both value-added and observation scores, we utilize the 100 to 400 point scale used by CPS for overall professional practice and student growth scores.

CHAPTER 2

Relationship between Teacher Characteristics and REACH Scores

In this chapter, we investigate the degree to which teachers' credentials (years of experience, advanced degree attainment, and National Board Certification) are associated with differences in their performance as measured by both value-added and observation scores.

In addition, we examine the relationships between teacher characteristics, such as a teacher's gender or race/ethnicity and evaluation scores. As discussed in the introduction, there are growing concerns about the changing composition of the overall teacher workforce in Chicago and elsewhere, as it has become whiter and less experienced over time. There are also far fewer male teachers in the district than female teachers (**see Table 2** for percentages of CPS teachers by race/ethnicity and gender). Previous research has shown that there are benefits for students when they have teachers like themselves, in terms of race and gender.[37] Evaluation scores are tied to high-stakes decisions such as dismissal, tenure attainment, and remediation. Thus,

there may be implications for the future diversity of the teacher workforce if such scores are related to teacher characteristics.

In Chapter 1, we found there were differences on evaluation scores by school characteristics. In Chapter 2, we present results adjusted for the schools teachers work in, as we want to understand differences by teacher characteristics and not school characteristics. However, because differences in scores that have not been adjusted for school characteristics may have meaningful consequences for teachers, we discuss unadjusted scores when they are substantially different from scores adjusted for school effects.

Years of Experience, Credentials, and Advanced Degrees

Teachers with more experience have slightly higher scores on both observations and value added in comparison to teachers in their first year of teaching. Comparing teachers within the same schools, there are only slight differences in value-added scores between teachers with few years of teaching experience and teachers with more years of experience. An exception is first-year teachers who have lower scores, on average, than teachers in any other experience category (**see Table 3**). On reading value-added, first-year teachers' scores were about seven points lower than teachers with 2-5 years of experience; on math value added the difference was about three points.

There are larger differences in observation scores between teachers with one year of experience and teachers with two years than there are in value-added scores. First-year teachers, on average, score 17 observation score points lower than teachers with 2-5years of experience. Thus, first-year teachers receive significantly lower ratings on both observations and value-

TABLE 2

2013-14 CPS Teachers Race/Ethnicity & Gender

	Number of Teachers	Percentage of Teachers
White	9,356	49%
African American	4,163	22%
Latino	3,606	19%
Other*	1,403	7%
Race/Ethnicity Unknown	510	3%
Female	14,286	77%
Male	4,242	23%
National Board Certified Teachers	1,462	8%
Teachers with Advanced Degrees	6,195	33%

*Other includes Asian, Hawaiian/Pacific Islander, Native American, and multi-racial.

---

37 Dee (2005); Ferguson (2003); Egalite et al. (2015).

TABLE 3

Years of Experience

Experience in the District	Average Scores Controlling for School Effects and Other Teacher Characteristics		
	Observation Score	Reading Value-Added Score	Math Valued-Added Score
1 Year	296.1	245.4	245.7
2-5 Years	312.7	251.9	248.5
6-10 Years	315.7	252.0	252.4
10-15 years	315.1	255.1	255.9
>15 Years	309.1	252.3	250.8

Note: The numbers on this table are predictions from a school fixed-effects regression model, representing comparisons of teachers with different experience levels who teach at the same school, controlling for National Board Certification, gender, and race/ethnicity. Bold indicates statistical significance (p>0.05) in comparison to first-year teachers. More details and unadjusted averages are available in Appendix G.

added scores than teachers with more than one year of experience.[38]

There are smaller differences among groups of teachers with more than one year of experience; teachers with more than 15 years of experience have slightly lower scores on both observation and value-added scores in comparison to teachers with 2-15 years of experience in the district. Using this data, we cannot say if these differences reflect teachers changing as they gain more experience, or teachers differing by cohort, or selective attrition among teachers.[39]

National Board Certification is a national teaching credential established by the National Board for Professional Teaching Standards (NBPTS) to signify the accomplishment of a high level of professional teaching.[40] Studies that explore the relationship between National Board Certification and value-added scores have been mixed; some studies have found evidence of small but significant effects of National Board Certified Teachers (NBCTs) on student achievement gains,[41] while other studies have found no evidence of differences between NBCT and non-NBCTs on value-added measures.[42] One study related observation scores to National Board Certification; scores were significantly higher for math teachers with board certification than those for teachers without that credential, but this difference was not significant in other subjects.[43]

REACH observation scores for NBCTs were 17 points higher than non-NBCTs, controlling for other teacher characteristics, such as tenure and advanced degree, and adjusting for school effects. However, there were no significant differences between NBCTs and non-NBCTs on value-added scores in either reading or math (see Table 4).[44]

---

38 Because first-year teachers are more likely to be teaching in high-poverty schools (see Appendix E), the adjustments for school factors may mask the overall difference in ratings for first-year teachers compared to others across the district—not just compared to teachers in the same school. In fact, we do find unadjusted differences in observation scores between first-year teachers and those with more experience to be slightly greater than the differences adjusted for school effects. On average, the unadjusted first-year teachers' observation scores are 24 points lower than those of teachers with 2-5 years of experience, while their reading value-added scores and math value-added scores are six and two points lower, respectively (see Table G.1 in Appendix G).

39 These data are cross-sectional. They denote teacher evaluation scores and years of experience in the district for 2013-14 and are not a comparison over time. Thus, we cannot and do not draw conclusions about teacher improvement over time,

as currently we have not accounted for attrition from the district or differences in teacher cohorts over time.

40 Teachers must submit extensive portfolios and pass a number of assessments. There is a 48 percent passage rate for those attempting certification. http://www.nbpts.org/

41 Goldhaber & Anthony (2007); Crofford, Pederson, & Garn (2014); Cowan & Goldhaber (2015); Cavalluzzo (2004).

42 Clotfelter et al. (2006); Harris & Sass (2011); Cantrell, Fullerton, Kane, & Staiger (2008).

43 Cavalluzzo, Barrow, & Henderson (2014).

44 On average, unadjusted for school effects, or teacher characteristics such as years of experience, the observation scores of NBCTs are 29 points higher than those of non-NBCTs, while there are no significant differences in both reading value-added scores and math value-added scores between NBCTs and non-NBCTs. See Table G.2 in Appendix G for raw averages.

Teachers with advanced degrees have slightly higher observation scores than those without; there are no significant differences in their value-added scores.[45] Research on the relationship between advanced degrees and value-added scores has found that having a higher degree is not associated with higher student achievement gains.[46] Teachers in CPS with advanced degrees scored five points higher on observation scores than those without when comparing teachers within the same school and controlling for other teacher characteristics. However, there were no significant differences between teachers with and without advanced degrees on either math or reading value added (see Table 4).

Teacher Gender and Race/Ethnicity

Previous studies relating teacher gender or race to their evaluation score are sparse as many districts are just beginning to generate new evaluation metrics. It is also difficult to parse whether differences by race/ethnicity and gender are due to differences in the classes or characteristics of students assigned to teachers of different races or genders.[47] In our analyses, we are able to adjust for the differences in schools in which teachers work, but not for the any differences in students or classes they are assigned within schools.

Male teachers have lower observation and value-added scores in comparison to female teachers. Male teachers had lower observation and value-added scores in comparison to female teachers with the same level of experience and credentials. Unadjusted for school effects, male teachers' observation scores were about 11 points lower, 2 points lower on math value added, and 5 points lower on reading value added (on a 100 to 400 point scale).[48]

There is little difference between average scores that have and have not been adjusted for school effects. Differences between male and female teachers on both observations and value-added scores remain significant after adjusting for school effects. On average, male teachers scored 12 points lower than female teachers on observations, about 4 points lower on math value added, and about 5 points lower on reading value added than their female counterparts within the same schools (see Table 5).

TABLE 4

National Board Certification & Advanced Degrees

	Average Scores Controlling for School Effects and Other Teacher Characteristics		
	Observation Scores	Reading Value-Added Score	Math Value-Added Score
Non-NBCTs	309.2	251.9	251.1
NBCTs	**325.8**	252.8	252.7
BA Only	307.4	251.0	250.3
Advanced Degree	**312.0**	252.4	251.7

Note: The numbers on this table are predictions from a school fixed-effects regression model representing comparisons of teachers with different credentials who teach at the same school, controlling for other teacher characteristics such as years of experience, gender, and race/ethnicity. Bold indicates statistical significance (p>0.05) in comparison to the excluded group (non-NBCTs or BA only). More details and unadjusted averages are available in Appendix G.

TABLE 5

Average Scores by Teacher Race/Ethnicity & Gender

	Average Scores Controlling for School Effects and Other Teacher Characteristics		
	Observation Scores	Reading Value-Added Score	Math Value-Added Score
Female	**313.1**	**252.6**	**252.2**
Male	301.6	247.9	247.7
White	314.5	252.2	251.6
African American	**304.5**	251.4	249.1
Latino	**308.0**	251.9	252.4
Other	**307.0**	252.4	255.0

Note: The numbers on this table are predictions from a school fixed-effects regression model representing comparisons of teachers with different credentials who teach at the same school, controlling for other teacher characteristics such as years of experience, gender, and credentials. Bold indicates statistical significance (p>0.05) in comparison to the excluded group (non-NBCTs or BA only). More details and unadjusted averages are available in Appendix G.

---

45 Currently we have not analyzed the specific fields of study of advanced degrees. Here, advanced degrees refer to any teachers with master's or doctoral degrees.

46 Clotfelter et al. (2006).

47 Paufler & Amrein-Beardsley (2013).

48 See Table G.3 in Appendix G for unadjusted averages.

Teachers from racial/ethnic minorities have lower observation scores than white teachers, but no significant differences on value added. As we have discussed in Chapter 1, observation scores and the level of student poverty at a school are related. The percentage of minority teachers and school-poverty level are also related. As the concentration of low-income students within a school increases, so does the percentage of teachers from racial/ethnic minorities. In lowest-poverty schools, 30 percent of teachers are from racial/ethnic minorities; in highest-poverty schools, 66 percent of teachers are from racial/ethnic minorities **(see Figure 5)**. The differences are especially distinct for African American teachers. In highest-poverty schools, almost 40 percent of teachers are African American; in the lowest-poverty schools, only 8 percent of teachers are African American.

If we do not take into account the differences in the types of schools in which teachers teach, African American teachers' observation scores were about 30 points lower on the observation scale (which ranges from 100-400 points), Latino teachers' observation scores were about 8 points lower, and other minority teachers were 10 points lower than non-minority teachers with similar levels of experience and credentials.[49]

However, the unadjusted differences do not account for the relationships between the percentage of minority teachers in a school and school characteristics. After adjusting for differences in schools, the differences in observation scores between teachers of racial/ethnic minorities and white teachers get smaller—especially for African American teachers. African American teachers scored 10 points lower than white teachers with similar levels of experience and credentials teaching in the same schools.[50] Latino teachers and other minority teachers scored about 7 points lower than white teachers with similar levels of experience teaching in the same schools **(see Table 5 on p.19)**.

Differences between African American teachers and white teachers' observation scores are largely driven by differences in schools; there are no significant differences in their value-added scores. The substantial difference between scores adjusted and unadjusted for school effects shows that a large proportion of the difference in observation scores between African American and white teachers is due to the substantial relationship between observation scores and school characteristics, such as school-level poverty, and the fact that African American teachers are overrepresented in the highest-poverty schools and underrepresented in the lowest-poverty schools.

There were no significant differences by teacher race/ethnicity on either reading or math value-added scores. This contrasts with what we find on observation scores. One possible explanation for the remaining differences between minority and white teachers within the same schools may be due to racial differences between the evaluator and teacher. However, in

FIGURE 5

Percentage of Teachers by Teacher Race/Ethnicity and School Poverty Level

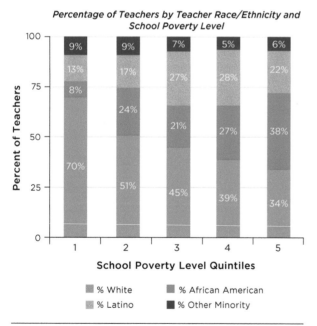

Percentage of Teachers by Teacher Race/Ethnicity and School Poverty Level

Note: Other includes Asian, Hawaiian/Pacific Islander, Native American, and multi-racial.

---

49 See Table G.3 in Appendix G for unadjusted averages.
50 We utilized a school fixed-effects model to compare teachers within the same school across all schools. See Appendix G for details.

CPS most African American teachers' evaluators were also African American. For example in 2013-14, about 75 percent of African American teachers' observations were conducted by African American evaluators.[51] Another possible explanation is that there are differences in the students assigned to minority and white teachers within the same schools. As discussed previously, value-added measures explicitly control for student characteristics such as economic disadvantage and previous achievement. There is research evidence that within schools minority teachers are assigned lower-achieving students than their white colleagues.[52] Thus it is possible the remaining differences on observation scores between minority and white teachers may be due to differences in the classrooms assigned to teachers within schools.

51 About 45 percent of white teachers' observations and 42 percent of Latino teachers' observations were conducted by an evaluator of the same race/ethnicity.
52 Kalogrides, Loeb, & Beteille (2012).

CHAPTER 3

Interpretive Summary

In this study, we find that schools with higher concentrations of disadvantaged students tend to have teachers with lower observation scores and teachers with lower value-added scores. This relationship is much more pronounced for observation scores than it is for the individual value-added scores of teachers in tested grades and subjects. We also find that schools with stronger culture and climate have higher teacher evaluation scores, even in schools with similar levels of poverty.

In addition, we find some differences in the relationships between evaluation scores and individual teacher background characteristics. Teachers in their first year of teaching typically have lower value-added and observation scores than their more experienced colleagues. NBCTs have higher observation scores than their colleagues as, to a lesser degree, do those with master's degrees; however, the value-added scores of NBCTs and of those with master's degrees are not different than those without such credentials. We also found that male teachers receive lower value-added and observation scores than female teachers. Teachers from racial/ethnic minorities receive lower observation scores than white teachers, although a large proportion of these differences can be attributed to the differences in characteristics of the schools in which they teach. There is no difference in value-added scores between teachers from racial/ethnic minority groups and white teachers.

We find observations have a much stronger relationship with school characteristics and some teacher characteristics than value added. Evaluation systems use multiple measures in order to capture different aspects of teacher performance. Value-added scores explicitly control for student characteristics such as previous achievement, student poverty, and mobility to compare a teacher's students to similar students district-wide.

Observations do not control for student characteristics; in fact the observation rubric utilized in Chicago (and in many districts) relies on evidence of not only the teacher's instruction but also of the students' engagement with that instruction. This evidence may reflect classroom characteristics—such as the previous achievement level of students in the class—and school wide policies—such as discipline and attendance outside of a teacher's control. This difference may help to explain why observation scores may have a stronger relationship with school characteristics and some teacher characteristics than value added.

This Report Leaves Many Unresolved Questions

This report presents a descriptive analysis of the relationships between teacher evaluation scores, their characteristics, and the context in which they teach, but it does not draw conclusions about why these relationships exist. We do know that these patterns are found not only in Chicago but also in districts across the nation.[53] We conclude by discussing critical gaps in the knowledge base on teacher evaluation and the questions raised by our findings.

1. On average, teachers at high-poverty schools receive lower observation scores than teachers at low-poverty schools. To what extent does this reflect true differences in teacher effectiveness or the sensitivity of observation scores to classroom or school contexts?

Since, on average, teachers at high-poverty schools receive lower observation scores than teachers at low-poverty schools, one key question that this report raises is whether they are actually providing less-effective instruction or whether observation based measures of teacher performance are influenced by the students they teach or the schools they serve.

23

---

53 See box entitled *Similar Findings in States and Districts Across the Nation* on page 11.

It is certainly possible that the lower observation scores in high-poverty schools indicate that students in those schools receive lower-quality instruction than students in schools with fewer disadvantages. The hallmark of the Distinguished rating, the highest level of practice on the Chicago Framework, is that teachers have been able to create a community of learners in which students assume a large part of the responsibility for the success of a lesson and their own learning.[54] However, past research suggests that students in many higher-poverty schools spend more time sitting and listening to scripted instruction rather than discussing, debating, and sharing ideas.[55] Furthermore, accountability pressures may increase focus on test preparation.[56] For over two decades, Martin Haberman has noted that a "pedagogy of poverty" exists in some high-poverty urban schools, where students experience a tightly controlled routine of teacher direction and student compliance—a pedagogy that is far different from *"the questioning, discovering, arguing, and collaborating"* that is more common among students in lower-poverty schools.[57]

In addition, teachers tend to prefer to work in schools where they are more likely to be effective.[58] Schools with more disadvantaged students have more difficulty recruiting teachers and experience higher turnover.[59] Thus over time, more effective teachers may be moving to lower-poverty schools.[60]

However, observation scores may also reflect the characteristics of students and schools. Teaching is an interaction among the teacher, the students, and the content within the context of schools.[61] The Danielson Framework for Teaching (on which Chicago's observation framework is based) is intended to explicitly capture classroom interactions; ratings rely on evidence of both the teacher's instruction and on the students' reactions to and engagement with that instruction. It is possible that the same teacher teaching the same lesson with the exact same instructional techniques may have very different results with one classroom of students versus another; those differences could result in different observation scores in the two classrooms. Furthermore, observation scores take place in a larger context: They may reflect that it is harder to get high scores in unorganized, chaotic schools or in schools with few resources or instructional supports for teachers, as other studies have shown.[62] There is emerging research evidence that finds characteristics of a teacher's students are related to a teacher's observation ratings; observation scores tend to be lower in classrooms of students with lower previous achievement.[63] One particular study concluded this is the result of bias in the observation scores against teachers who are assigned less able and prepared student and recommended statistically adjusting observation scores for the background characteristics of the students in the classroom.[64]

2. Why do we see differences in observation scores by gender, race, and ethnicity?

A second important question that this report does not answer is why, on average, minority teachers get lower observation scores than their white colleagues, even though we see no significant differences in their value-added scores. We see that a substantial proportion of the difference on the observation scores between white and minority teachers is due to minority teachers disproportionately teaching in high-poverty schools since, on average, teachers in high-poverty schools get lower observation scores than teachers in low-poverty schools. This report does not address the extent to which there may be further systematic differences in how students are assigned to teachers, which may also help explain these differences. For example, minority or male teachers may be assigned more students with

54 Danielson (2011).
55 Smith, Lee, & Newmann (2001); Diamond & Spillane (2004); Anyon (1980); Knapp, Turnbull, & Shields (1990).
56 Diamond & Spillane (2004); Taylor, Shepard, Kinner, & Rosenthal (2001).
57 Haberman (1991); Haberman (2010).
58 Simon & Moore-Johnson (2015); Lankford et al. (2002); Hanushek, Kain, & Rivkin (2001).
59 Boyd, Grossman, Lankford, Loeb, & Wyckoff (2008); Allensworth, Ponisciak, & Mazzeo (2009); Goldhaber, Gross, & Player (2010); Guarino, Santibañez, & Daley (2006); Hanushek, Kain, & Rivkin (2001); Scafidi, Sjoquist, & Stinebricker (2007).
60 Kalogrides & Loeb (2013).
61 Cohen, Raudenbush, & Ball (2003).
62 Cohen, Mccabe, Michelli, & Pickeral (2009); Hargreaves (1997).
63 Whitehurst et al. (2014), Steinberg & Garrett (forthcoming).
64 Whitehurst et al. (2014).

discipline issues, or with previous low achievement or special education status. If so, it is possible this might negatively impact what an observer sees in their classroom and therefore what score they are assigned.

This report also does not address the extent to which evaluators' characteristics may be related to observation scores. For example, do the ratings of evaluators who are of the same race/ethnicity and/or gender as the teachers differ from the ratings assigned by evaluators who are different with respect to gender or race/ethnicity? Does the age of the evaluator relative to the age of the teacher have an impact on teachers' scores? In Chicago, evaluators can only be the school principal or assistant principal; the principal's prior knowledge and relationship with their teachers may influence their ratings.[65] It may also be possible that principals inflate their ratings at the high-end of the scale as other studies have found.[66] Furthermore, the report does not answer whether the reliability or validity of an evaluator's observation ratings are related to school characteristics.

We plan to address some of these questions in future reports.

3. In general, students in high-poverty schools are more likely to be taught by teachers with lower observation and value-added scores. What are some possible ways to ensure all students have equal access to high-quality education?

The district's most disadvantaged students are more likely to have teachers with lower observation and value-added scores. However, the findings in this report also show there is a greater difference in teacher scores within schools than there is across schools. In other words, teachers with high observation and high value-added scores are found in almost all schools. Thus, in even the highest-poverty schools, there are teachers with high scores.

In fact, on value added we see that the best teachers in the highest-poverty schools have the best scores in the district. While it is possible that teachers with the highest ratings are also those who teach the strongest students within a school, it is also likely these teachers have skills

and dispositions that enable them to be effective in the most challenging of circumstances. School and district leaders need to leverage the strengths of these teachers, ensure their talents remain in the district and enable other teachers to learn from them.

Our findings also indicate that schools with stronger culture and climate have higher teacher evaluation scores, even in schools with similar levels of poverty. Better understanding of how to build strong school organizational climate in our highest-need schools may be a step in creating environments where teachers can be successful. It is possible that districts will not be able to improve student-learning gains without improvements in schools and more understanding of the structural issues affecting high-poverty schools and disadvantaged students such as housing, health, and crime.

New Evaluation Systems Have Potential but There Is a Need for Continuous Improvement

REACH represents a dramatic change from the previous checklist system, which was widely regarded as superficial and perfunctory and provided little to no information about teachers.[67] REACH utilizes multiple measures, and the use of these measures presents advantages and disadvantages. First, these measures may offer some transparency into differences in teacher scores by school types and by teacher background characteristics. Having multiple measures allows districts and policymakers to compare and contrast measures and further diagnose issues with each measure and also capture different aspects of instruction.

However, there continue to be questions about whether teacher evaluation measures—both value added and observations—accurately capture teacher quality. Differences in observation scores may have implications for the teacher workforce.

In Chicago, as in most districts and states, observations make up the bulk of a teacher's overall evaluation score. The lower observation scores of teachers who teach in higher-poverty schools may add additional disincentives to working in higher-poverty schools or

65 Sartain, Stoelinga, & Brown (2011); Jacobs (2010).
66 Sartain et al. (2011).

67 Weingartern (2010).

with disadvantaged students. In addition, if minority teachers are more likely to work in contexts where it is difficult to get high ratings, the composition of the workforce itself could be affected by the personnel decisions based on evaluation scores. This is especially true for African American teachers, who disproportionately teach in higher-poverty schools.

To account for the influence of student characteristics on teacher observation scores, some researchers have recommended adjusting teacher observation scores for the demographic characteristics of their classrooms for high stakes accountability decisions such as dismissal or also gather further evidence such as additional observations across difference classrooms.[68]

Others suggest that observation scores should utilize multiple years of teacher data or should include observations of multiple classes within the same year to adjust for differences in classroom composition.[69]

In our previous reports, we found teachers and administrators in CPS remain positive about the new evaluation system's potential to drive instructional change. Teachers are particularly positive about the observation process and the opportunity for feedback, reflection, and communication it provides. Designing and implementing evaluation systems is an ongoing process that is important for districts and policymakers to continue to improve the design of these systems to leverage their strengths and mitigate issues.

68 Whitehurst et al. (2014).
69 Steinberg & Garrett (forthcoming).

References

Aaronson, D., Barrow, L., & Sander, W. (2007)
Teachers and student achievement in the Chicago public high schools. *Journal of Labor Economics, 25*(1), 95-135.

Albert Shanker Institute (2015)
The state of teacher diversity in American education. Washington, DC: Albert Shanker Institute.

Allensworth, E., Ponisciak, S., & Mazzeo, C. (2009)
The schools teachers leave: Teacher mobility in Chicago Public Schools. Chicago, IL: University of Chicago Consortium on Chicago School Research.

Anyon, J. (1980)
Social class and the hidden curriculum of work. *Journal of Education, 162*(1), 67-92.

Boyd, D., Grossman, P., Lankford, H., Loeb, S., & Wyckoff, J. (2008)
Who leaves? Teacher attrition and student achievement. NBER Working Paper No. 14022. Cambridge, MA: National Bureau of Economic Research. Retrieved from http://www.nber.org/papers/w14022.

Bryk, A.S., Sebring, P.B., Allensworth, E., Luppescu, S., & Easton, J.Q. (2010)
Organizing schools for improvement: Lessons from Chicago. Chicago, IL: University of Chicago Press.

Cantrell, S. Fullerton, J., Kane, T.J. & Staiger, D.O. (2008)
National Board Certification and teacher effectiveness: Evidence from a random assignment experiment. Washington, DC: National Board for Professional Teaching Standards.

Cavalluzzo, L. (2004)
Is National Board Certification an effective signal of teacher quality? Alexandria, VA: The CAN Corporation.

Cavalluzzo, L., Barrow, L., & Henderson, S. (2014)
From large urban to small rural schools: An empirical *study of National Board Certification and teaching effectiveness.* Arlington, VA: CNA Analysis and Solutions.

Chetty, R., Friedman, J.N., & Rockoff, J.E. (2011)
Measuring the Impacts of Teachers II: Teacher Value-Added and Student Outcomes in Adulthood. *American Economic Review,* American Economic Association, vol. 104(9), pages 2633-2679.

Chicago Public Schools. (2014)
REACH students: Educator evaluation handbook, 2014-2015. Chicago, IL: Chicago Public Schools.

Clotfelter, C.T., Ladd, H., & Vigdor, J.L. (2006)
Teacher-student matching and the assessment of teacher effectiveness. *Journal of Human Resources, 41*(4), 778-820.

Cohen, D., Raudenbush, S.W., & Ball, D.L. (2003)
Resources, instruction and research. *Educational Evaluation and Policy Analysis, 25*(2), 119-142.

Cohen, J., McCabe, E.M., Michelli, N.M., & Pickeral, T. (2009)
School climate: Research, policy, practice, and teacher education. *Teachers College Record 111*(1), 180-213.

Cowan, J, & Goldhaber, D. (2015)
National Board Certification and teacher effectiveness: Evidence from Washington. Seattle, WA: Center for Education Data & Research.

Crofford, G.D., Pederson, J.E., & Garn, G. (2014)
Exploring the relationship between National Board Certification and high school student achievement. *New Horizons for Learning, 9*(1).

Danielson, C. (2011)
Enhancing professional practice: A framework for teaching (2nd ed.). Alexandria, VA: Association for Supervisions and Curriculum Development

DeAngelis, K.J., Presley, J.B., & White, B.R. (2005)
The distribution of teacher quality in Illinois. Edwardsville, IL: Illinois Education Research Council.

Dee, T.S. (2005)
A teacher like me: Does race, ethnicity, or gender matter? *American Economic Review, 95*(2), 158–165.

Diamond, J.B., & Spillane, J.P. (2004)
High-stakes accountability in urban elementary schools: Challenging or reproducing inequality? *Teachers College Record, 106*(6), 1145-1176.

Education Consortium for Research and Evaluation. (2013)
Evaluation of the DC Public Education Reform Amendment Act (PERAA). Washington, DC: Office of the District of Columbia Auditor.

Egalite, A.J., Kisida, B., & Winters, M.A. (2015)
Representation in the classroom: The effect of own-race teachers on student achievement. *Economics of Education Review, 45,* 44-52.

Ferguson, R.F. (2003)
Teachers' perceptions and expectations and the Black-White test score gap. *Urban Education, 38*(4), 460-507.

Goldhaber, D. (2002)
The mystery of good teaching. *Education Next, 2*(1), 50-55.

Goldhaber, D. & Anthony, E. (2007)
Can teacher quality be effectively assessed? National Board Certification as a signal of effective teaching. *Review of Economics and Statistics, 89*(1), 134-150.

Goldhaber, D., Gross, B., & Player, D. (2010)
Teacher career paths, teacher quality, and persistence in the classroom: Are public schools keeping their best?. *Journal of Policy Analysis and Management, 30*(1), 57-87.

Goldhaber, D., Lavery, L, & Theobald, R. (2015)
Uneven playing field? Assessing the teacher quality gap between advantaged and disadvantaged students. *Educational Researcher, 44*(5), 293-307.

Government Accountability Office. (2013)
Race to the Top: States implementing teacher and principal evaluation systems despite challenges. Washington, DC: United States Government Accountability Office.

Grissom, J.A., Loeb, S., & Master, B. (2013)
Effective instructional time use for school leaders: Longitudinal evidence from observations of principals. *Educational Researcher, 42*(8), 433-444.

Guarino, C., Santibanez, L., & Daley, G. (2006)
Teacher recruitment and retention: A review of the recent empirical literature. *Review of Educational Research, 72*(2), 173–208.

Haberman, M. (1991)
The pedagogy of poverty vs good teaching. *Phi Delta Kappan, 73*(4), 290-294.

Haberman, M. (2010)
Eleven consequences of failing to address the 'pedagogy of poverty.' *Phi Delta Kappan, 92*(2), 45.

Hanushek, E.A., Kain, J.F., & Rivkin, S.G. (2001)
Why public schools lose teachers. Greensboro, NC: Smith Richardson Foundation.

Hargreaves, A. (1997)
Cultures of teaching and educational change. In B.J. Biddle et al. (Eds), *International Handbook of Teachers and Teaching* (pp. 1297-1319). Netherlands: Springer Science+Business Media B.V.

Harris, D., & Sass, T. (2011)
Teacher training, teacher quality, and student achievement. *Journal of Public Economics, 95*(7-8), 798-812.

Jacob, B. (2010)
Do principals fire the worst teachers? NBER Working Paper 15715. Cambridge, MA: National Bureau of Economic Research. Retrieved from http://www.nber.org/papers/w15715.pdf

Jiang, J.Y., & Sporte, S.E. (2014)
Teacher evaluation in practice: Year 2 teacher and administrator perceptions of REACH. Chicago, IL: University of Chicago Consortium on Chicago School Research.

Jiang, J.Y., Sporte, S.E., & Luppescu, S. (2014)
Analytic memo: Evaluation data from the first year of REACH. Chicago, IL: University of Chicago Consortium on Chicago School Research.

Jiang, J.Y., Sporte, S.E., & Luppescu, S. (2015)
Teacher perspectives on evaluation reform: Chicago's REACH students [Special issue]. *Educational Researcher, 44*, 105-116

Kalogrides, D., & Loeb, S. (2013)
Different teachers, different peers: The magnitude of student sorting within schools. *Educational Researcher, 42*(6), 304-316.

Kalogrides, D., Loeb, S., & Beteille, T. (2012)
Systematic sorting: Teacher characteristics and class assignments. *Sociology of Education*, 1-21.

Knapp, M.S., Turnbull, B.J., & Shields, P.M. (1990)
New directions for educating the children of poverty. *Educational Leadership, 48*(1), 4-8.

Lankford, H., Loeb, S., & Wyckoff, J. (2002)
Teacher sorting and the plight of urban schools: A descriptive analysis. *Educational Evaluation and Policy Analysis 24*(1), 37–62.

Matos, A. (2015, January 28)
Minneapolis' worst teachers are in the poorest schools, data show. *Star Tribune.* Retrieved from http://www.startribune.com/nov-2-minneapolis-worst-teachers-in-poorest-schools-data-show/281191231/

Moore, N. (2015, July 14)
Why are there fewer black teachers in CPS? *WBEZ 91.5.* Retrieved from http://www.wbez.org/news/why-are-there-fewer-black-teachers-cps-112385

Murphy, H., Cole, C., Pike, G., Ansaldo, J., & Robinson, J. (2014)
Indiana teacher evaluation: At the crossroads of implementation. Bloomington, IN: Indiana Institute on Disability and Community.

National Council on Teacher Quality (2013)
State of the States 2013 Connect the Dots: Using evaluations of teacher effectiveness to inform policy and practice. Washington, DC: National Council on Teacher Quality.

Paufler, N.A.& Amrein-Beardsley, A. (2013)
The random assignment of students into elementary classrooms: Implications for value-added analyses and interpretations. *American Educational Research Journal*, 1-35.

Raudenbush, S.W., & Bryk, A.S. (2002)
Hierarchical linear models: Applications and data analysis methods (2nd ed). Newbury Park, CA: Sage.

Rivkin, S.G., Hanushek, E.A., & Kain, J.F. (2005)
Teachers, schools, and academic achievement. *Econometrica, 73*(2), 417-458.

28

Rockoff, J.E. (2004)
The impact of individual teachers on student achievement: Evidence from panel data. *American Economic Review, 94*(2), 247-252.

Sartain, L., Stoelinga, S.R., Brown, E., Luppescu, S., Matsko, K.K., Miller, F.K., Durwood, C., Jiang, J.Y., & Glazer, D. (2011)
Rethinking teacher evaluation in Chicago: Lessons learned from classroom observations, principal-teacher conferences, and district implementation. Chicago, IL: University of Chicago Consortium on Chicago School Research.

Sass, T., Hannaway, J., Xu, Z., Figlio, D., & Feng, L. (2010)
Value added of teachers in high-poverty schools and lower-poverty schools. CALDER Working Paper No. 52. Washington, DC: National Center for Analysis of Longitudinal Data in Education Research. Retrieved from http://myweb.fsu.edu/tsass/Papers/Hi%20Lo%20Poverty%20003.pdf

Scafidi, B., Sjoquist, D.L., & Stinebrickner, T.R. (2007)
Race, poverty, and teacher mobility. *Economics of Education Review, 26*(2),145-159.

Sebastian, J., & Allensworth, E. (2012)
The influence of principal leadership on classroom instruction and student learning: A study of mediated pathways to learning. *Educational Administration Quarterly, 48*(626), 626-663.

Simon, N., & Moore-Johnson, S. (2015)
Teacher turnover in high-poverty schools: What we know and can do. *Teachers College Record, 117*(3), 1-36.

Smith, J.B., Lee, V.E., & Newmann, F.M. (2001)
Instruction and achievement in Chicago Elementary Schools. Chicago, IL: University of Chicago Consortium on Chicago School Research.

Sporte, S., Stevens, W.D., Healey, K., Jiang, J., & Hart, H. (2013)
Teacher evaluation in practice: Implementing Chicago's REACH Students. Chicago, IL: University of Chicago Consortium on Chicago School Research.

Steinberg, M.P., & Donaldson, M. (2014)
The new Educational accountability: Understanding the landscape of teacher evaluation in the post-NCLB era. Policy brief. Storrs, CT: University of Connecticut Center for Education Policy Analysis.

Steinberg, M. & Garrett, R. (forthcoming)
Classroom composition and measured teacher performance: What do teacher observation scores really measure? *Educational Evaluation and Policy Analysis.*

Steinberg, M., & Sartain, L (2015)
Does teacher evaluation improve school performance? Experimental evidence from Chicago's excellence in teaching project. *Education Finance and Policy, 10*(4), 535-572.

Taylor, E.S. & Tyler, J.H. (2012)
The effect of evaluation on teacher performance. *American Economic Review, 102*(7): 3628-3651.

Taylor, G., Shepard, L., Kinner, F., & Rosenthal, J. (2003)
A survey of teacher's perspectives on high-stakes testing in Colorado: What gets taught, what gets lost. CSE Technical Report. Los Angeles, CA: National Center for Research on Evaluation, Standards, and Student Testing.

U.S. Department of Education. (2001)
Laws & guidance/elementary and secondary education: Qualifications for teachers and paraprofessionals, Public Law 107-110, Section 1119. Retrieved from http://www2.ed.gov/policy/elsec/leg/esea02/pg2.html#sec1119

U.S. Department of Education. (2009)
Race to the Top program executive summary. Retrieved from http://www2.ed.gov/programs/racetothetop/executive-summary.pdf

Weingarten, R. (2010)
The professional educator: A new path forward: Four approaches to quality teaching and better schools. *American Educator, 12*, 36-39.

Whitehurst, G.J., Chingos, M.M., & Lindquist, K.M. (2014)
Evaluating teachers with classroom observations: Lessons learned in four districts. Washington, DC: Brown Center on Education Policy at Brookings.

Appendix A
2013-14 REACH Scores and Ratings

A teacher's REACH score is comprised of a professional practice score and up to two measures of student growth (performance tasks and value added). For more details on REACH, visit **http://www.cps.edu/reachstudents**.

Professional Practice

Teachers are evaluated over multiple classroom observations using the CPS Framework for Teaching, a modified version of the Charlotte Danielson Framework for Teaching (**see Appendix B for Framework**). Formal observations last at least 45 minutes and include pre- and post-observation conferences. Currently in CPS, only principals and assistant principals can be certified evaluators. To be assigned a summative REACH evaluation rating, a teacher must be observed four times. Non-tenured teachers[70] and tenured teachers with previous low ratings[71] are observed four times annually and receive a REACH rating each year. Tenured teachers with previous high ratings are observed four times over the course of two years and receive a summative REACH rating every two years since, under Illinois law, tenured teachers are evaluated every two years.

Student Growth

To meet Illinois state law requirements about which assessments must be used for teacher evaluation, CPS has identified two different types of student assessments.

Value-Added Measures

Teachers who teach grades 3-8 reading and/or math receive an individual value-added score based on their students' NWEA MAP—an adaptive, computer-based test.

For high school teachers in core subjects, CPS started using the EPAS suite of tests (EXPLORE, PLAN, and ACT) in the 2013-14 school year. However high school value added only counted as 5 percent of a teacher's overall REACH score in 2013-14 for teachers in tested subjects and grades. High school value-added scores were not utilized in 2014-15. Thus, our analyses in this report do not include high school value added.

Performance Tasks

Developed by teams of CPS teachers, teams within individual schools, and/or central office staff, performance tasks are written or hands-on assessments designed to measure the mastery or progress toward mastery of a particular skill or standard. Performance tasks are typically administered and scored by teachers once at the beginning of the year and once at the end of the school year.

REACH Scores and Ratings

Professional practice scores are combined with student growth scores for an overall REACH score, which ranges from 100 to 400 and translates to a REACH rating of Unsatisfactory, Developing, Proficient, or Excellent (**see Table A.1**). The percentages assigned to professional practice and the measures of student growth for different groups of teachers are detailed in **Table A.2**.

TABLE A.1

REACH Ratings

REACH Score	Rating
100 – 209	Unsatisfactory
210 – 284	Developing
285 – 339	Proficient
340 – 400	Excellent

---

70 Teachers in CPS typically attain tenure in their fourth year in the district.

71 Tenured teachers with previous low ratings include those who received an Unsatisfactory or Satisfactory rating on the previous system. Tenured teachers missing previous ratings were to receive four observations and a REACH rating in 2013-14 and then be placed on a biennial cycle in the following year.

TABLE A.2

REACH Measures

Educators	2012-13			2013-14			2014-15		
	Professional Practice	Student Growth		Professional Practice	Student Growth		Professional Practice	Student Growth	
	Observations	Performance Tasks	Value Added	Observations	Performance Tasks	Value Added	Observations	Performance Tasks	Value Added
Elementary Educators Who Teach Grades 3–8 English, Reading, and/or Math	75%	10%	15% Individual	75%	10%	15% Individual	70%	10%	20% Individual
Elementary Pre-K—Grade 2 Educators	75%	15%	10% School-Wide	75%	25%		70%	30%	
Elementary Grades 3–8 Educators of Non-Tested Subjects	75%	15%	10% School-Wide	75%	15%	10% School-Wide	70%	20%	10% School-Wide
High School Educators Who Teach English, Math, Science, and/or Social Science*	90%	10%		75%	20%	5% Individual	70%	30%	
High School Educators Who Do Not Teach English, Math, Science, and/or Social Science	100%			75%	20%	5% School-Wide	70%	30%	
Counselors, Related Service Providers (RSP), Educational Support Specialists (ESS)	100%			100%			100%		

Note: In 2012-13 high school educators in core subjects had performance task scores. Summative REACH scores for high school educators in non-core subjects were based 100 percent on observations.

Appendix B
The CPS Framework for Teaching

The CPS Framework for Teaching

Adapted from the *Danielson Framework for Teaching* and Approved by Charlotte Danielson

Domain 1: Planning and Preparation

a. Demonstrating Knowledge of Content and Pedagogy
Knowledge of Content Standards Within and Across Grade Levels
Knowledge of Disciplinary Literacy
Knowledge of Prerequisite Relationships
Knowledge of Content-Related Pedagogy

b. Demonstrating Knowledge of Students
Knowledge of Child and Adolescent Development
Knowledge of the Learning Process
Knowledge of Students' Skills, Knowledge, and Language Proficiency
Knowledge of Students' Interests and Cultural Heritage
Knowledge of Students' Special Needs and Appropriate
   Accommodations/Modifications

c. Selecting Instructional Outcomes
Sequence and Alignment
Clarity
Balance

d. Designing Coherent Instruction
Unit/Lesson Design that Incorporates Knowledge of Students and
   Student Needs
Unit/Lesson Alignment of Standards-Based Objectives, Assessments,
   and Learning Tasks
Use of a Variety of Complex Texts, Materials and Resources, including
   Technology
Instructional Groups
Access for Diverse Learners

e. Designing Student Assessment
Congruence with Standards-Based Learning Objectives
Levels of Performance and Standards
Design of Formative Assessments
Use for Planning

Domain 2: The Classroom Environment

a. Creating an Environment of Respect and Rapport
Teacher Interaction with Students, including both Words and Actions
Student Interactions with One Another, including both Words and
   Actions

b. Establishing a Culture for Learning
Importance of Learning
Expectations for Learning and Achievement
Student Ownership of Learning

c. Managing Classroom Procedures
Management of Instructional Groups
Management of Transitions
Management of Materials and Supplies
Performance of Non-Instructional Duties
Direction of Volunteers and Paraprofessionals

d. Managing Student Behavior
Expectations and Norms
Monitoring of Student Behavior
Fostering Positive Student Behavior
Response to Student Behavior

Domain 4: Professional Responsibilities

a. Reflecting on Teaching and Learning
Effectiveness
Use in Future Teaching

b. Maintaining Accurate Records
Student Completion of Assignments
Student Progress in Learning
Non-Instructional Records

c. Communicating with Families
Information and Updates about Grade Level Expectations and Student
   Progress
Engagement of Families and Guardians as Partners in the Instructional
   Program
Response to Families
Cultural Appropriateness

d. Growing and Developing Professionally
Enhancement of Content Knowledge and Pedagogical Skill
Collaboration and Professional Inquiry to Advance Student Learning
Participation in School Leadership Team and/or Teacher Teams
Incorporation of Feedback

e. Demonstrating Professionalism
Integrity and Ethical Conduct
Commitment to College and Career Readiness
Advocacy
Decision-Making
Compliance with School and District Regulations

Domain 3: Instruction

a. Communicating with Students
Standards-Based Learning Objectives
Directions for Activities
Content Delivery and Clarity
Use of Oral and Written Language

b. Using Questioning and Discussion Techniques
Use of Low- and High-Level Questioning
Discussion Techniques
Student Participation and Explanation of Thinking

c. Engaging Students in Learning
Standards-Based Objectives and Task Complexity
Access to Suitable and Engaging Texts
Structure, Pacing and Grouping

d. Using Assessment in Instruction
Assessment Performance Levels
Monitoring of Student Learning with Checks for Understanding
Student Self-Assessment and Monitoring of Progress

e. Demonstrating Flexibility and Responsiveness
Lesson Adjustment
Response to Student Needs
Persistence
Intervention and Enrichment

2012

33

Appendix C
Methods for Analyzing Relationships between REACH Scores and School Characteristics

We find, descriptively, observation scores have a negative relationship with our school-level measures of student poverty, percent minority, and previous achievement. As the concentration of poverty within a school increases, teacher observation scores decrease on average.

There is a weaker relationship between school-level measures of student poverty and teacher value-added scores, as value added explicitly controls for student poverty and other characteristics.

Observation data analyzed in this report are from 2013-14 and are described on page 8. Only teachers with at least two observations were included in our analysis of observation scores. Value-added data analyzed in this report are from 2012-13 and 2013-14, as we utilized multi-year averages for teachers when available. We utilized a two-level hierarchical linear model, controlling for teacher characteristics at level 1 and school characteristics at level 2. Our outcomes were professional practice scores (the weighted average of a teacher's observation component ratings) and individual value-added scores.

Level 1 Model:

$$Y_{ij} = \beta_{0j} + \beta_1 \text{Tenure}_{ij} + \beta_2 \text{AdvancedDegree}_{ij} + \beta_3 \text{NBCT}_{ij} + r_{ij}$$

Level 2 Model:

$$\beta_{0j} = \gamma_{00} + \gamma_{01} \text{LogEnrollment}_j + \gamma_{02} X_j + u_{0j}$$

where:

Y is one of three outcomes (observation score and math and reading value-added scores) for teacher i in school j. X are our school-level characteristics of interest and each one is included in our model in separate regressions. The coefficient of interest is γ_{02}, which is the association between our outcomes (observation and value-added scores) and school-level characteristics (concentration of poverty, previous achievement, percent minority). Table C.1 presents coefficients from models predicting teachers' observation scores and Table C.2 presents coefficients from models predicting teachers' value-added scores. School-level percentage African American students is an indicator for schools with greater than 70 percent African American students.

TABLE C.1

The Association between Observation Scores and School Characteristics

Observation Score	Elementary				High School			
	Model 1	Model 2	Model 3	Model 4	Model 1	Model 2	Model 3	Model 4
School-Level Concentration of Student Poverty	-14.688***				-20.076***			
School-Level Percentage FRL		-12.482***				-9.584***		
School-Level Percentage African American Students			-30.922***				-24.553***	
School-Level Previous Achievement				14.190***				13.096**

Note: The coefficients shown in this table are from regressions of observation scores with school characteristics controlling for teacher characteristics (tenure status, advanced degree, National Board Certification) and school size. Asterisks denote statistical significance: *** at the 0.01 level, ** at the 0.05 level, and * at the 0.10 level. All predictors are z-standardized except the school-level percentage of African American students.

We utilized two measures of economic status of students in schools. The first is the percentage of students eligible for free/reduced-price lunch in a school. The second, the concentration of student poverty, is derived from census data on students' residential neighborhoods, measured at the census block group level (but averaged at the school level) and captures the percent of unemployed males over 16 and the percent of families with incomes below the poverty line. **Table C.3** shows summary statistics of these two measures of school-level poverty.

Previous school-average achievement is calculated differently depending on the schools' grade configuration.

Elementary Schools: We ran a three-level hierarchical linear model (HLM) using ISAT test scores from 2012-13 as the outcome. We included a measurement model at level 1, individuals at level 2, and schools at level 3.[72] In level 2, we included dummy variables indicating the student's grade, with grade 6 the omitted grade. Thus, the school-level empirical Bayes estimates represent the predicted average achievement for the students in grade 6, adjusted for the grade structure of the school, and the amount of measurement error in the test scores.

TABLE C.2

The Association between Value-Added Scores and School Characteristics

Reading Value Added Elementary	Model 1	Model 2	Model 3	Model 4
School-Level Concentration of Student Poverty	-2.307**			
School-Level Percentage FRPL		-1.731*		
School-Level Percentage African American Students			0.1470	
School-Level Previous Achievement				5.438***
Math Value Added Elementary	Model 1	Model 2	Model 3	Model 4
School-Level Concentration of Student Poverty	1.807			
School-Level Percentage FRL		0.667		
School-Level Percentage African American Students			3.241	
School-Level Previous Achievement				2.644**

Note: The coefficients shown in this table are from regressions of value-added scores with school characteristics controlling for teacher characteristics (tenure status, advanced degree, National Board certification) and school size. Asterisks denote statistical significance: *** at the 0.01 level, ** at the 0.05 level, and * at the 0.10 level. All predictors, except the school-level percentage of African American students, are z-standardized.

TABLE C.3

Measures of School-Level Poverty

		Mean	STD	Min	Max	Number of Schools
Percent Free/Reduced-Price Lunch	ELEM	0.835	0.228	0.101	1	425
	HS	0.857	0.154	0.308	0.995	101
SCON	ELEM	0.237	0.569	-1.097	2.20	425
	HS	0.331	0.404	-0.616	1.074	101

---

72 Raudenbush & Bryk (2002).

High Schools: We used the average incoming student achievement level of ninth-graders in the 2012-13 freshman cohort for each school. This was calculated using a longitudinal three-level HLM with test scores from 2006-07 to 2011-12 as the outcome. Each student's test score trajectory was calculated separately for math and reading, including the student's year in school, and the year squared, centered on grade 5. The student's eighth-grade test score as predicted by the model is the incoming achievement. It takes into consideration the student's entire test score history and levels the effects of random measurement error in individual test scores.

Correlations between our measures of school-level poverty and observation scores are similar for each of the four domains of the CPS Framework for teaching.

TABLE C.4

REACH Scores Correlation with Measures of School-Level Concentration of Poverty

	Correlation with Measures of Concentration of Economically Disadvantaged Students	
	School-Level Concentration of Student Poverty	School-Level Percentage FRL
Domain 1	-.3012	-.2160
Domain 2	-.3082	-.2068
Domain 3	-.3228	-.2359
Domain 4	-.2717	-.1839
Observation Score	-.3346	-.2374
Reading Value-Added Score	-.0471	-.0468
Math Value-Added Score	.0450	.0161

Appendix D
Math and Reading Value-Added Scores and High School Observation Scores by School-Level Poverty

Figures D.1, D.2, and D.3 display the distribution of teachers with the highest scores (top 20 percent) and lowest scores (bottom 20 percent) on reading value added and math value added for elementary schools and high school observation scores across differing levels of school poverty (quintiles of school-level poverty). In these figures, school-level poverty is measured by the percentage of students eligible for free/reduced-price lunch.

For example, 18 percent of teachers with top scores on reading value added are in schools with lowest poverty and 18 percent of teachers with top scores on reading value added are in highest-poverty schools. Teachers with bottom scores on reading value-added (bottom 20 percent) are overrepresented in highest-poverty schools. Twenty-six percent of teachers with lowest scores on reading value added are in highest-poverty schools while only 13 percent are in lowest-poverty schools.

In high schools 45 percent of teachers with top scores on observations are in schools with lowest poverty and only 4 percent are in schools with highest poverty. Teachers with lowest scores on observations are slightly overrepresented in highest-poverty schools.

FIGURE D.1

Teachers with Lowest Reading Value-Added Scores are Over Represented in Highest Poverty Schools

Distribution of Teachers with the Highest and Lowest Reading Value-Added Scores by School Poverty Level

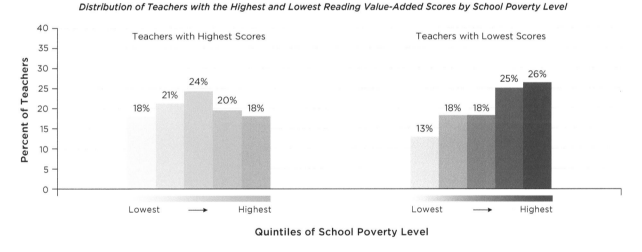

Note: Elementary school only. 2,609 lowest-rated teachers and 2,594 highest-rated teachers.

Teachers with Highest and Lowest Math Value-Added Score are More Evenly Distributed Among Schools

Distribution of Teachers with the Highest and Lowest Math Value-Added Scores by School Poverty Level

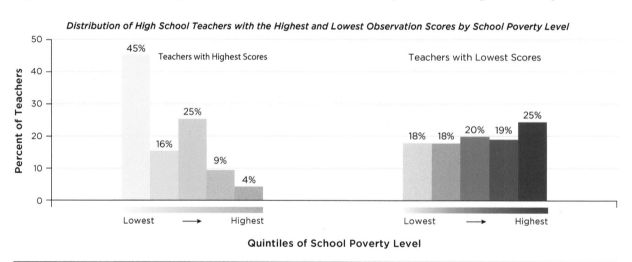

Note: Elementary school only. 2,609 lowest-rated teachers and 2,594 highest-rated teachers.

High School Teachers with Highest Observation Scores are Under Represented in Highest-Poverty Schools

Distribution of High School Teachers with the Highest and Lowest Observation Scores by School Poverty Level

Note: High school only. 985 lowest-rated teachers and 996 highest rated teachers.

Appendix E
Percentages of First-Year Teachers and National Board Certified Teachers by School Poverty Level

Figures E.1 and E.2 display the distribution of new teachers and teachers with National Board Certification across schools with differing levels of school poverty (quintiles of school-level poverty). In these figures, school-level poverty is measured by the percentage of students eligible for free/ reduced-price lunch. **Figure E.1** shows that highest-poverty elementary and high schools tend to have higher percentages of first-year teachers. **Figure E.2** shows that highest-poverty elementary and high schools tend to have lower percentages of teachers with National Board Certification.

FIGURE E.1

Percentages of First-YearTeachers in Each School-Poverty Quintile

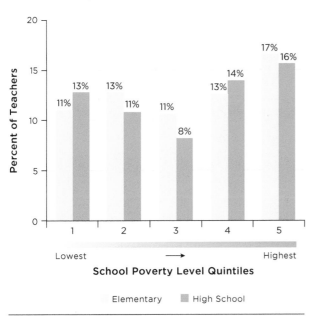

Note: Elementary schools 1700 new teachers. High schools, 606 new teachers. New teachers defined as teachers with <1.5 years of experience in the district.

FIGURE E.2

Percentages of NBCTs in Each School-Poverty Quintile

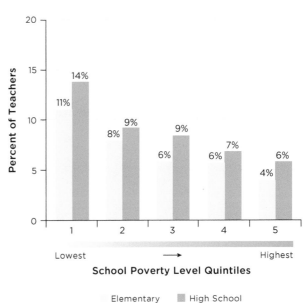

Note: Elementary schools: 973 NBCT teachers. High schools: 488 NBCT teachers.

Appendix F
Change to Models Utilized for Analysis of the Relationships between REACH Scores and Measures of School Climate

In Chapter 1, we examined relationships between the climate and culture of schools and the observation and value-added scores of teachers in those schools utilizing student and teacher perceptions of climate and culture from the district wide *My Voice, My School* surveys from the spring of 2014.

In schools with stronger professional climate—as perceived by teachers—and stronger learning climate and instruction—as perceived by students—teachers tend to have higher scores on both value-added and observation scores. To analyze these relationships, we utilized a two-level hierarchical linear model, controlling for teacher characteristics at level 1 and school characteristics such as poverty, percentage minority, and previous achievement at level 2. Our outcomes were professional practice scores (the weighted average of a teacher's observation score) and individual value-added scores. We included each survey measure of school climate in separate regressions to avoid colinearity issues.

Level 1 Model:

$$Y_{ij} = \alpha_{0j} + \Sigma \alpha K_{ij} + r_{ij}$$

Level 2 Model:

$$\alpha_{0j} = \lambda_{00} + \lambda_{01} R_j + \Sigma \lambda N_j + u_{0j}$$

where:

Y is one of three outcomes (observation score, math value-added score, and reading value-added score) for teacher i in school j. K is a vector of teacher characteristics (years of experience, gender, race/ethnicity, advanced degree) for teacher i in school j. N is a vector of school characteristics (e.g., school-level poverty, previous achievement) for school j.

R represents our survey measures of school climate; each one is included in our model as separate regressions. The coefficient of interest is λ_{01}, which is the association between our outcomes (observation and value-added scores) and school-level measures of climate. These coefficients are presented in **Tables F.1)**

REACH Scores and Survey Measures of School Climate

Survey Measures	Observations	Reading Value Added	Math Value Added
	Coefficient	Coefficient	Coefficient
Academic Personalism (Student)	1.531	3.714***	3.561***
Academic Press (Student)	1.842	4.314***	4.162***
Collective Responsibility (Teacher)	4.080***	4.419***	3.397***
Outreach to Parents (Teacher)	3.958***	4.937***	3.427***
Peer Support for Academic Work (Student)	2.161*	4.544***	4.097***
Principal Instructional Leadership (Teacher)	3.812***	4.74***	4.152***
Program Coherence (Teacher)	4.723***	3.903***	2.926**
Quality of Student Discussion (Teacher)	5.555***	4.399***	2.719**
Quality Professional Development (Teacher)	3.399***	4.495***	2.770**
Safety (Student)	4.791***	3.858***	1.843
School Commitment (Teacher)	8.144***	4.867***	3.135**
Socialization of New Teachers (Teacher)	5.185***	3.475***	2.370**
Student Responsibility (Teacher)	6.072***	5.567***	3.965**
Student-Teacher Trust (Student)	1.709	3.057***	2.231**
Teacher Influence (Teacher)	7.284***	3.0315***	2.871**
Teacher Safety (Teacher)	-5.508***	-7.959***	-6.289***
Teacher-Parent Trust (Teacher)	3.879***	4.163***	2.234*
Teacher-Principal Trust (Teacher)	6.675***	2.692***	2.325**
Teacher-Teacher Trust (Teacher)	1.744	1.412	1.190

Note: Teacher Safety is a negatively valenced measure where higher values indicate teachers feeling less safe.

41

Appendix G
Models Utilized for Analysis of Teacher Background Characteristics and Evaluation Scores

In Chapter 2, we examined relationships between observation scores, value-added scores, and teacher background characteristics (years of experience, advanced degree, National Board Certification, teacher race/ethnicity, and teacher gender).

To analyze these relationships, we utilized a school fixed-effect model comparing teachers within the same schools across all schools.

$$Y_{ij} = \beta_1 X_{ij} + \alpha_j + \varepsilon_{ij}$$

where:

Y is one of two outcomes (observation score and value-added score) for teacher i in school j.

X represents our variables of interest (years of experience, gender, race/ethnicity, advanced degree) for teacher i in school j. The associations for each predictor are estimated in separate models. All predictors are categorical; for those with more than two categories we entered a series of dummy variables in the model.

β_1 is the coefficient for a particular teacher background characteristic (listed above).

α_j are fixed-effects for each school j.

TABLE G.1

Years of Experience

Experience in the District	Unadjusted Average Scores		
	Observation Score	Reading Value-Added Score	Math Value-Added Score
1 Year	291.7	244.1	250.9
2-5 Years	**315.2**	**249.8**	252.5
6-10 Years	**317.1**	**250.2**	252.1
10-15 years	**313.6**	**251.9**	252.0
>15 Years	**307.4**	**249.0**	247.4

Note: Unadjusted average scores are raw averages not adjusting for other teacher characteristics or school effects. Bolded indicates a statistical significant difference from first-year teachers (p>0.05).

Advanced Degrees and National Board Certification

	Unadjusted Average Scores		
	Observation Score	Reading Value-Added Score	Math Value-Added Score
Non-NBCTs	307.3	248.7	250.0
NBCTs	**336.4**	253.1	252.7
BA Only	305.0	247.7	250.1
Advanced Degree	**313.2**	250.1	251.0

Note: Unadjusted average scores are raw averages not adjusting for other teacher characteristics or school effects. Bolded indicates a statistical significance difference with excluded group (non-NBCTs or BA only) at p>0.05.

Average Scores by Teacher Race/Ethnicity and Gender

	Unadjusted Average Scores		
	Observation Score	Reading Value-Added Score	Math Value-Added Score
Male	301.8	245.0	248.9
Female	**312.9**	**250.2**	251.1
White	319.0	248.9	251.3
African American	**289.3**	249.6	249.9
Latino	**311.7**	244.3	248.9
Other	**309.7**	252.7	254.6

Note: Unadjusted average scores are raw averages not adjusting for other teacher characteristics or school effects. Bolded indicates a statistical significant difference with excluded group (male for gender, white for race/ethnicity) at p>0.05.

ABOUT THE AUTHORS

JENNIE Y. JIANG is a Senior Research Analyst at UChicago Consortium. She is currently working on a study of charter high schools, in addition to her work on teacher evaluation. Previously, she was a teacher in both Chicago Public Schools and in Shenzhen, China. She earned an MPP in public policy at the University of Chicago and an MS in education at Northwestern University. Jiang's research interests include teacher preparation, quality and support, school leadership, and school choice.

SUSAN E. SPORTE is Director of Research Operations at UChicago Consortium. Her current research focuses on teacher preparation, measuring effective teaching, and schools as organizations. She serves as main point of contact with Chicago Public Schools regarding data sharing and research priorities; she also oversees UChicago Consortium's data archive. Sporte received a BS in mathematics from Michigan State University, an MA in mathematics from the University of Illinois at Springfield, and an EdM and EdD in administration, planning, and social policy from the Harvard Graduate School of Education.

This report reflects the interpretation of the authors. Although UChicago Consortium's Steering Committee provided technical advice, no formal endorsement by these individuals, organizations, or the full Consortium should be assumed.